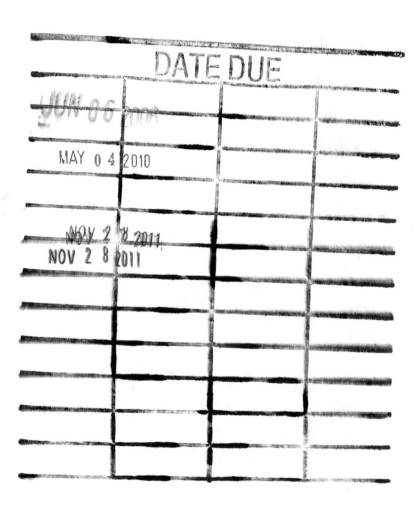

Collective Biographies

AMERICAN LEGENDS OF ROCK

Ron Knapp

 Enslow Publishers, Inc.

40 Industrial Road	PO Box 38
Box 398	Aldershot
Berkeley Heights, NJ 07922	Hants GU12 6BP
USA	UK

http://www.enslow.com

Library of Congress Cataloging-in-Publication Data

Knapp, Ron.
    American legends of rock / Ron Knapp.
       p. cm. — (Collective biographies)
    Includes bibliographical references and index.
    Summary: Profiles the lives of ten rock and roll artists, including Elvis
Presley, Bruce Springsteen, Jimi Hendrix, Aretha Franklin, and the Beach
Boys.
    ISBN 0-89490-709-3
    1. Rock musicians—United States—Biography—Juvenile literature.
[1. Musicians. 2. Rock music.] I. Title. II Series.
ML3929.K6 1996
781.66'092'2—dc20
    [B]   .   96-5269
                                     CIP
                                 AC MN

Printed in the United States of America.

10 9 8 7 6 5 4 3

Photo Credits: DEL-FI Records, Inc., p. 40; Frank Driggs Collection,
pp. 8, 12, 16, 22, 26, 31, 36, 44, 47, 54, 60, 94, 99; Elektra
Entertainment, pp. 74, 80; The Jimi Hendrix Exhibition/Gered
Mankowitz, p. 88; Allen Koss/MCA Records, p. 84; Rhino Records, pp.
64, 69.

Cover Photo: AP Photo/Paul Chiasson

Contents

Introduction

"Rock and roll music is basically gospel and rhythm and blues," said Elvis Presley. "It sprang from that, and people have been adding to it . . . experimenting with it."[1]

Gospel and rhythm and blues have their roots in the African music brought to America by black slaves. As they worked in the fields of the South, they sang the songs they remembered from their homelands. The African influence was responsible for the driving beat, the shouting, and the clapping that marked the music of the black church.

The slaves' songs developed into gospel music and blues. By the 1940s, her strong, dignified style had made Mahalia Jackson the world's most popular gospel singer. Blues music was usually mournful songs about life's troubles. W. C. Handy wrote the first great blues in the first decades of the twentieth century. Muddy Waters, the "King of Chicago Blues," later recorded songs like "I Can't Be Satisfied" and "I'm Your Hoochie Coochie Man" with his slide guitar. When blues music was speeded up on the piano, the new sound was called boogie-woogie. When it was played with a beat on different instruments, it became known as rhythm and blues.

The whites of the rural South were singing, too, backed with banjos, mandolins, and dulcimers. Many of their songs were slow, high-pitched ballads about love and guilt. By the early 1900s, their melodies and lyrics had developed into bluegrass and country music. On songs like "Your Cheatin' Heart," Hank Williams's clear, sweet voice made him a country superstar before his death in a 1953 car crash.

In the 1950s, young stars like Joan Baez and the Kingston Trio popularized folk music, simple tunes usually accompanied by acoustic guitars and banjos. Woody Guthrie had written some of the best folk music decades before. His travels during the Great Depression led to songs like "This Land Is Your Land" and "Pretty Boy Floyd." More than any other type of music, folk songs addressed social problems like wars, racial prejudice, and poverty.

In the early 1950s, these different types of music began coming together as something exciting and new. A disc jockey in Cleveland, Alan Freed, popularized the term rock and roll. Besides playing the new music on his radio program, he organized some of the earliest rock concert tours. Most of the music was played on electric guitars.

The first big rock and roll hits were written and sung by black artists. Since record companies didn't believe white teenagers would buy music by black artists (they called it "race music"), they rerecorded the songs with white peformers. Joe Turner's "Shake,

Rattle & Roll" was made popular by Bill Haley and the Comets. Little Richard's "Long Tall Sally" and Fats Domino's "Ain't That a Shame" were taken by Pat Boone.

Chuck Berry was one of the first black artists to have a large white following. He and Buddy Holly, a young white singer from Texas, wrote and sang many of rock and roll's classic songs in the 1950s. At the same time, Elvis Presley was exploding onto the scene. Ever since then, American artists have dominated rock and roll music. Even the great British groups like the Beatles and the Rolling Stones, who appeared in the 1960s, began their careers singing songs by Berry and Holly.

Of course, rock and roll has evolved since Berry, Presley, and Holly. The Beach Boys made sweet harmonies popular a few years before artists like Jimi Hendrix and the Doors introduced different, harsher sounds. Soul music, Aretha Franklin's version of rhythm and blues, arrived late in the 1960s. Bob Dylan and Bruce Springsteen focused attention on the words behind the music. More recently, new styles like disco and rap have developed.

Through the years, rock and roll has been most popular with the young. Older people found something sinister and disgusting in Elvis's dancing, Dylan's lyrics, and the hard beat that drives most rock and roll songs. Teenagers, for their part, almost always seem to enjoy music their parents hate.

The first great rock music was recorded on

seven-inch vinyl records called 45s because they went around the turntable forty-five times a minute. There was enough room for one song on each side. Since 1955, *Billboard* magazine has compiled weekly charts of the nation's most popular single songs. Of course, today, cassettes and compact discs have replaced records.

But no matter how it is recorded, rock and roll has remained the world's most popular music. This book tells the story of some of the talented artists—composers, instrumentalists, and singers—who helped make rock what it is today.

Chuck Berry

Chuck Berry

Roll Over Beethoven

When Charles Edward Anderson Berry was born on October 18, 1926, in St. Louis, Missouri, Calvin Coolidge was president of the United States.[1] By the time he became a rock and roll star in the 1950s, Berry was a generation older than the teenagers who bought his records.

His own teenage years weren't happy ones. Berry was arrested for car theft and spent more than three years in a reformatory. Upon his release, he stayed out of trouble, getting a license in hairdressing and cosmetology. He got married and earned a decent living as an autoworker and a beautician in St. Louis.

When he wasn't working, he enjoyed playing his guitar, but usually it was just for himself and his family. It wasn't until he was twenty-six years old that he had his first paying gig. Once he became comfortable on stage, he began developing his own style of music. Between songs made popular by blues guitarist Muddy Waters and the jazz-pop singer Nat King Cole, he played country tunes.

In 1955, Berry went to Chicago to see a performance by Waters. The blues star invited him to play, and was so impressed he sent him to Chess Records for an audition. Soon Chuck had a recording contract.

At his first session, he played "Wee Wee Hours," a blues tune, and "Ida Red," a song that sounded part country, part rhythm and blues. Berry liked "Wee Wee Hours" best, but Chuck Chess, president of the company, thought "Ida Red" was a bouncy, catchy song that would sell a lot of records. "It was something new," he said. "I liked it. I told Chuck to give it a bigger beat. . . . The kids wanted the big beat, cars, and young love."[2] The only thing Chess didn't like about "Ida Red" was the title. He suggested "Maybellene."

To make sure the record was a big seller, he asked disc jockey Alan Freed to play it regularly on his popular radio program. Freed agreed, but he demanded to be listed as the song's cowriter. That meant he would share in the money it made. Soon "Maybellene" was the No. 5 hit in the country.

No matter who got the credit, Berry's streak of great early rock and roll songs was beginning. "Roll Over Beethoven" told classical music fans there was a new kind of music on the scene. Even though by then Berry was more than thirty years old, "Sweet Little Sixteen" and "School Days" captured the spirit of being a teenager. "Johnny B. Goode" seemed to be Berry's own theme song. His audiences sang along, begging him and his guitar to "go, go, go." "Rock and Roll Music" was a rousing anthem for his fans.

In the mid-1950s there was nobody else like Chuck Berry. His driving, aggressive music was exciting and new. In the past, guitarists had played in the background while somebody else sang. Berry changed all that by standing up front and playing while he sang. At the same time, he was also moving and dancing. At one of Freed's shows in Brooklyn, New York, he first performed his famous "duckwalk." With one leg extended in front of him, he hopped across the stage on the other, without missing a lick on his guitar. Berry's showmanship made guitar-playing cool, and the guitar became the symbol of rock and roll.

But he was not popular with everybody. Older people, who didn't like rock and roll anyway, were especially unhappy that the work of a black musician was being enjoyed by white teenagers. He was arrested for bringing a fourteen-year-old girl to work in his club. Authorities charged that she was his girlfriend, and he served twenty months in the Indiana Federal Penitentiary.

Many of Berry's detractors hoped that his stay in jail would destroy his popularity. However, his music remained in the spotlight, largely because it had

Chuck Berry was one of the first guitarists to stand up front and play while he sang.

been discovered by two new English groups. The Beatles recorded "Rock and Roll Music" and "Roll Over Beethoven." One of the Rolling Stones' earliest singles was "Come On," another Berry song. While he was in jail, Chess released *Chuck Berry on Stage,* an album of his greatest hits rerecorded with clapping, cheering fans.

After his release in 1964, Berry had a pair of hits, "No Particular Place to Go" and "You Can Never Tell." He left Chess for a $50,000 advance and a new contract from Mercury Records, but the hits stopped coming. He continued to record, but his songs didn't sell. However, because his old music continued to be popular, he played successfully all over the United States and Europe.

At the 1972 Arts Festival in Lanchester, England, he played "My Ding-a-Ling," a silly, slightly dirty song. The audience loved it—and so did almost everybody else when it was released as a single. It seemed ironic that a man who had written classic rock and roll songs couldn't reach No. 1 on the singles charts until he recorded "My Ding-a-Ling."

In 1979, Chuck released his last album, *Rockit,* but it sold very poorly. That was the same year he was in trouble again with the law, this time for income tax evasion. He was convicted and served five months at Lompoc Prison Farm in California.

It wasn't until the 1980s that Berry's achievements in music were generally recognized. At the 1985 Grammy Awards, he received a Lifetime Achievement

Award. The next year he was inducted as a charter member into the Rock and Roll Hall of Fame. Two of his songs, "Maybellene" and "Roll Over Beethoven," made it into the Grammy Hall of Fame. Keith Richards, the Rolling Stones' guitarist, organized a concert to celebrate Berry's birthday in 1988. The festivities were filmed and released as a movie, *Hail! Hail! Rock 'n' Roll.*

Despite the controversy that has sometimes marked his career, nobody can disagree with the fact that Chuck Berry's music has gone farther than that of any other rock and roll musician. In 1978, the Voyager 2 spacecraft was launched to take photographs of the planets Jupiter and Saturn. When its photographic mission was over, it sailed past the planets and out of the solar system. If there is intelligent life in outer space, the first evidence they will get of life on Earth will be the Voyager.

Scientists attached some diagrams and a metal disc to the spacecraft. On the disc are recorded music by Johann Sebastian Bach, messages from people all over the world—and Chuck Berry's version of "Johnny B. Goode."

Suggested Recordings

Is On Top (Chess, 1959)
St. Louis to Liverpool (Chess, 1964)
Great Twenty-eight (Chess, 1982)
Chess Box (Chess, 1988)

Elvis Presley

Elvis Presley

The King of Rock

For his eleventh birthday in 1946, Elvis Aron Presley wanted his parents, Vernon and Gladys, to buy him a bicycle. But Elvis's mother was worried. Would the young boy really be safe riding a bike through the streets of tiny Tupelo, Mississippi? She always kept a close eye on Elvis. Until he was a teenager, she walked him to school every day. She talked him into a safer—and cheaper—present, a $12.98 guitar.

Soon after he got the guitar, Elvis and his parents left Tupelo, where he had been born on January 8, 1935. At his new home in Memphis, Tennessee, he was able to enjoy the feeling and excitement of gospel music. When he was a teenager, he and his friends sneaked out of the back row of their church on Sundays so they could listen to the choir sing at a black church a short drive away.

Elvis never learned to play his guitar very well. When he was a star, he joked that his playing sounded like "someone beating on a bucket lid."[1] But he had a great voice and he loved music.

The way his hair looked was always very important to Presley. He once convinced his mother to give his dark blond hair a curly permanent. Another time he shocked his friends by having most of his head shaved into a Mohawk style. When he was sixteen, he discovered a thick grease that could keep his unruly hair in place. It also darkened it and made it shine. He combed and greased his hair very carefully so that a thick lock was free to dangle down on his forehead. To finish off the new look, he let his sideburns grow to the bottoms of his ears.

Most of his classmates at Hume High School in Memphis thought Presley's slicked-down hair looked very strange, and they made fun of him. Once four or five football players trapped him in the boys' room. "They were holding him and pushing him up against the wall," said Red West, another classmate. "They were yelling and laughing and wising off at him and his hair. They decided that they were gonna cut his hair." West felt sorry for Elvis. "He was looking like a frightened little animal." He told the bullies to leave his friend alone, and Elvis's hair was saved.[2]

A month after graduating from high school,

Presley got the nerve to make a record at a studio in Memphis. It only cost $3.98, and he was anxious "to hear what I sounded like." When the studio's secretary asked, "Who do you sound like?" he answered, "I don't sound like nobody."[3] He recorded two slow ballads, "My Happiness" and "That's When Your Heartaches Begin," then walked out with his record.

The owner of the little studio was Sam Phillips. He knew that white teenagers would love the rollicking, exciting sound of black singers, but unless the songs were sung by whites, they would never buy the records. Racial discrimination was still prevalent in the 1950s. Very few blacks appeared in movies or on television programs. Only a few gifted black athletes, like Jackie Robinson in baseball, had managed to break into the major leagues.

Many times Phillips said, "If only I could find a white man who had the Negro sound and the Negro feel, I could make a billion dollars."[4] Almost a year after Presley had visited the studio, his secretary asked, "What about the kid with the sideburns?"[5]

When Elvis came to the studio on July 5, 1954, at first he sounded like just another ballad singer. Then, when everybody else was taking a break, "Elvis started singing a song, jumping around and just acting the fool," said guitarist Scotty Moore. Soon the other musicians joined in. Phillips stuck his head in the door and asked, "What are you doing?" Presley and the others shook their heads and said, "We don't know." For a few seconds, they thought they were in trouble. Then Phillips said, "Well, back up, try to find a place to start, and do it again."[6]

The song was "That's All Right," a blues tune that Elvis had just turned into a rock and roll song. Within a few weeks, his record was being played on a Memphis radio station. The disc jockey was careful to point out that Presley had graduated from Hume High, a white school.

For a year, Phillips continued to record his new star in between concerts throughout the South. Then Elvis signed with RCA, a national company, and his music became known throughout the world. He wailed his way through "Heartbreak Hotel," the sad story of a lonely man who had lost his "baby." It was No. 1 for eight weeks in the spring of 1956. In the summer came "Hound Dog," with lyrics that didn't make much sense, but a strong beat and Presley's growling vocals. With "Don't Be Cruel" on the flip side, it was No. 1 for eleven weeks. "Love Me Tender," a beautiful slow romantic tune, was next, on top of the charts for five weeks.

It wasn't just his music that was making Elvis popular. It was also his style and his attitude. Bob Lumen, a country singer, saw one of Presley's early concerts in Kilgore, Texas: "The cat came out in red pants and a green coat and a pink shirt and socks, and he had this sneer on his face. He stood behind the mike for five minutes, I'll bet, before he made a move. Then he hit his guitar a lick, and he broke two strings. So there he was, these two strings dangling, and he hadn't done anything yet, and these high school girls were screaming and fainting and running to the stage. Then he started to move his hips. . . . He made chills run up my back, man."[7]

As he sang onstage, his legs shook and his arms fluttered. He grabbed the microphone, bent down almost to the stage, then shook it and dragged it back and forth. He went down in the splits or on one knee. Sometimes he dove to the stage and crawled on his belly, reaching for the audience. Many adults thought his performances were disgusting, but his fans loved them. "When I sing this rock 'n' roll," he said, "my eyes won't stay open and my legs won't stand still. I don't care what they say, it ain't nasty."[8]

Elvis Presley had suddenly become the most famous young man in the world. "My daddy and I were laughing about it the other day," he said in 1956. "He looked at me and said, 'What happened, El? The last thing I can remember is I was working in a can factory, and you were driving a truck.'"[9]

The hits kept coming. Most of them were rockers like "Too Much," "All Shook Up," "Teddy Bear," and "Jailhouse Rock," but there were also a few slow ones like "Don't." His career was interrupted for two years when he was drafted into the Army in March 1958, but Presley's fans were loyal. Four days after becoming a civilian again, he was

Elvis's good looks and stage presence appealed to many teenagers in the 1950s. Though his dancing is tame by today's standards, it alarmed many adults at that time.

back in the recording studio. Before anybody had heard his next single or even knew its title, more than 1,200,000 copies had been ordered. It was "Stuck on You," No. 1 for four weeks in the spring of 1960.

When he was released from the Army, Presley no longer seemed to upset adults. Many of them respected him for serving his country, and they liked his new appearance. The pink and green suits were gone. So were the sideburns. His hair was shorter, and it didn't look as wild as it did at the beginning of his career. His music changed, too; it wasn't as loud or as fast as his early records. "Are You Lonesome Tonight?," a No. 1 hit in 1960, was a slow ballad that had first been recorded thirty-four years before. Soon Elvis gave up concerts to concentrate on movies. Most of his music from the mid-1960s came from the soundtracks to those films. Although the movies made him a lot of money, many teenagers quit buying his records. They were more interested in the new sounds coming from groups like the Beatles, the Rolling Stones, and the Doors.

In 1968, Presley decided he didn't want to be left behind. He took a break from movies to make *Elvis,* a television special. From the opening of the show when he sang, "Looking for trouble? You came to the right place," it was obvious he still knew how to rock.[10] Wearing a tight leather suit copied from Jim Morrison, he sang all his hits to a wildly cheering audience. He closed the show with "If I

Can Dream," an inspiring tune that didn't sound anything like his bland movie music.

Within a few months, Elvis was back on top with "Suspicious Minds," his first No. 1 song in seven years—and his last. He returned to the concert stage in Las Vegas and in arenas around the country, but in the 1970s his music suffered as he fought losing battles against obesity and drug use. He died of a heart attack on August 16, 1977.

When he was a little boy and his family was very poor, Elvis had told his mother, "Don't you worry none, baby. When I grow up, I'm going to buy you a fine house . . . and get two Cadillacs—one for you and Daddy, and one for me.'"[11]

Of course he did all that—and more. He bought a fleet of Cadillacs and lived in a mansion called Graceland, which is still visited every day by thousands of fans. He was the biggest rock and roll star of all. More than any other performer, he made rock and roll the most popular music in the world. As Buddy Holly pointed out, "Without Elvis, none of us would have made it."[12]

Suggested Recordings

Elvis Presley (RCA, 1956)
Elvis (RCA, 1956)
Elvis Television Special (RCA, 1968)
Collector's Gold (RCA, 1971)
Sun Sessions (RCA, 1976)
Reconsider Baby (RCA, 1985)
Top Ten Hits (RCA, 1987)
Memphis Record (RCA, 1987)
King of Rock 'n' Roll: Complete 50's Masters
(RCA, 1992)
From Nashville to Memphis: The Essential 60's
Masters (RCA, 1993)

Buddy Holly

Buddy Holly
The Day the Music Died

When Charles Hardin Holley was five years old, he didn't care much about music. When there was a talent show near his home in Lubbock, Texas, in 1941, he had to be convinced to go onstage. Carrying a toy violin, he sang "Down the River of Memories," a tune his mother had taught him. He was good enough to win a $5 prize.

Even when he was a little boy, nobody called him Charles Hardin. His parents figured that "it was too long a name for such a little boy." Soon after his birth on September 7, 1936, in Lubbock, Texas, everybody began calling him "Buddy."[1]

The little boy didn't think much more about music until he was eleven years old. Since his older brothers, Larry and Travis, could already play instruments, Mrs. Holley decided it was time for Buddy to learn, too. He began taking piano lessons, and his teacher said he was one of her best pupils. However, after nine months, he decided he had had enough. He wanted to learn to play the guitar instead.

So the Holleys bought him an acoustic guitar, and Travis taught him a few chords. After that, Buddy was on his own, and he became quite good on the new instrument. Country music was what he listened to on the radio, and that's what he liked to play, especially songs by Hank Williams. His favorite song was "Lovesick Blues." Sometimes he played it for his friends as they rode the bus to school.

When he was in seventh grade, he met a classmate who could also play the guitar. Soon he and Bob Montgomery became Buddy and Bob, a country music duo. One of their first performances was at a parents' night program at their junior high school. They dedicated a song to their teachers: "Too Old to Cut the Mustard." Mrs. Holley wished they had picked another tune. "Oh, we were so embarrassed," she said. "We felt like sinking right into the ground."[2]

When they were in high school, Buddy and Bob got their own radio show on KDAV, a small new station in Lubbock. The boys, now backed by a bass player, played for a half hour every Sunday afternoon. Montgomery usually sang on country songs, but Holley was the singer when they did rockabilly and rhythm and blues. The boys surprised many of their listeners when they played music made popular by a wild new country singer named Elvis Presley.

Buddy met Elvis when he came to Lubbock in 1955 to sing at a country dance hall and for the opening of a car dealership. He and Montgomery talked with Elvis while he drank a soda at the club. "You know, he's a real nice, friendly fellow," Holley told a friend.[3] A few months later when Presley returned for another performance, they gave him a guided tour of Lubbock.

Of course, Buddy and Bob continued to perform in clubs and at dances. They wanted the same kind of success Elvis was beginning to enjoy. By then, Holley was developing a unique vocal style. His voice slid back and forth from deep bass to high falsetto. The way he clipped his words and popped them quickly out of his mouth almost made it sound like he was hiccuping. He also had his own style on the guitar. Almost everybody played the instrument by strumming back and forth with a pick. Buddy didn't strum back and forth; he hit the strings only on the way down. That meant he had to move his fingers twice as fast to play the same beat.

More and more, Buddy and Bob were leaving the country sound behind and sticking with rockabilly. Most of the time, Montgomery just played the guitar. In January 1956, Buddy was offered a recording contract as a solo act. Holley didn't want to break up his group, but Bob said, "You've got your chance—now go ahead."[4] Buddy lost his partner—and the *e* in his last name when it was misspelled in his contract. As a professional musician, he would be known as Buddy Holly.

At first, his records didn't sell, and it didn't look like his career was going anywhere. It got so bad that Buddy called an old friend who ran a club in Amarillo, Texas. "We're hungry," he said. So the manager gave Holly and his new band Friday bookings at the club. They didn't earn much for the gig, but the manager let them eat free at his restaurant.[5]

Because of some legal questions about the recording contracts he'd signed, Buddy's band needed a name. In 1957, a noisy cricket ruined several takes at a recording session. Holly and the others stopped singing and playing to search for the pesky insect. When they couldn't find it, they resumed recording, and the cricket resumed chirping. For a while, it seemed as if it was chirping along to the beat of the music. Buddy decided to call his band the Crickets.[6]

Tough guy actor John Wayne gave Holly the idea for his first hit single.[7] In the movie *The Searchers,* Wayne said, "That'll be the day." Buddy made the line the title of a song about a guy who didn't want his girlfriend to leave him. It was first recorded in July 1956 for Decca Records, but the company didn't think it was good enough to be released. The next year, after switching to Coral/Brunswick Records, he recorded the song again and "That'll Be the Day" went to No. 1. Finally, Buddy was a star.

Soon he wrote a new song about a girl named

Buddy Holly and the Crickets (left to right, Sonny Curtis, Jerry Alison, Buddy, and Don Guess), were radio favorites in the 1950s with songs like "Rave On," "That'll Be the Day," and "Peggy Sue."

"Cindy Lou." In the recording studio, Jerry Allison, one of the Crickets, suggested that he change the title to "Peggy Sue," the name of Allison's girlfriend. With Holly's clipped, repeated phrases and a driving beat, the song became another big hit.

As their records began to sell, Buddy Holly and the Crickets began to appear on television and in concerts all over the United States and Europe. Many of his fans were surprised when they first saw him. He was the first popular performer to wear glasses on stage. Of course, he didn't really have a choice. Contact lenses were not yet available, and without his thick glasses, he was afraid he might step off the edge of the stage. Early in his career, he wore glasses with thin, light frames. Allison told him that was a mistake. "If you're going to wear glasses, then really make it obvious that you're wearing glasses."[8] Holly switched to the thick, dark, square frames that became his trademark.

In the 1950s, rock and roll stars rarely appeared in concerts as solo acts. Instead they played in shows with several other artists. Then they rode in buses overnight to get to another city for another show. Buddy toured with some of the biggest names in the record business—Fats Domino, Jerry Lee Lewis, the Everly Brothers, Paul Anka, and Little Richard. On one of his earliest tours, Buddy and Chuck Berry spent their nights kneeling in the back of the bus, playing cards.

By late 1958, Holly wanted to quit touring for a

while, so he could spend time with his new wife, Maria Elena, and write some new music. Unfortunately, he needed money, so in January 1959, he began the Winter Dance Party tour with Ritchie Valens, the Big Bopper, Dion and the Belmonts, and Frankie Sardo. The Crickets didn't go, and Waylon Jennings, who would later become a big country star, was one of the musicians hired to back him. The weather was cold, the drives between cities were long, and the bus had no heat. After a concert in Clear Lake, Iowa, on February 2, Holly chartered a small airplane. When it crashed early the next morning, he was killed, along with the other three men in the plane: the Big Bopper, Valens, and the pilot.

Buddy Holly was only twenty-two when he died, but he was one of rock music's most influential early stars. In his moving song, "American Pie," Don McLean calls the night Buddy's plane crashed, "the day the music died." As the rock critic Malcolm Jones pointed out, Holly was the first rock musician to use strings and double track his voice. The Crickets were the first white band to have drums and three guitars (rhythm, bass, and lead).[9]

When they began singing in England, John Lennon and Paul McCartney imitated Buddy Holly on "Words of Love" and other songs he wrote.[10] When they needed a name for their group, they paid tribute to the Crickets by calling themselves the Beatles.[11]

One of the Rolling Stones' first singles was another Holly song, "Not Fade Away." That's the song they used to open their 1994–95 Voodoo Lounge tour in stadiums and arenas around the world.

In *Rock Encyclopedia,* Lillian Roxon wrote that Holly "was one of the giants of early rock, a figure so important in the history of popular music that it is impossible to hear a song on the charts today that does not owe something to the tall, slim, bespectacled boy from Lubbock, Texas."[12]

Suggested Recordings

For the First Time Anywhere (MCA, 1983)
From the Original Master Tapes (MCA, 1985)
Something Special From Buddy Holly
(Rollercoaster, 1986)
Buddy Holly Collection (MCA, 1993)

Ritchie Valens

4

Ritchie Valens
La Bamba

Shortly after his birth on May 13, 1941, in Los Angeles, Ritchie Valenzuela's family knew he loved music. When he was three, his mother, Concepcion, watched him try to make a guitar out of a tin can and some rubber bands. Two years later, he had better luck using a cigar box.

His father, Steve, encouraged him to learn to play the guitar and the trumpet. He also loved to hear his son sing, but Ritchie was shy. At parties, Steve Valenzuela forced the little boy to perform. Sometimes he threatened to spank him with a belt if he wouldn't sing.

When he was growing up in California, Ritchie enjoyed the music of singing cowboys like Gene Autry and Roy Rogers. He also sang the Spanish songs his Mexican-American family enjoyed. By the time he was a teenager in the 1950s, his favorite performer was Little Richard, one of the earliest and most flamboyant rock and roll singers.

As he got better on the guitar, Ritchie started to enjoy performing. At Pacoima Junior High School, he was kidded a lot because he was heavy, but when he was singing nobody seemed to pay any attention to his weight. He began carrying his guitar to school and playing it between classes and at lunch. His classmates enjoyed the way he added funny lyrics to popular songs. One of their favorites was "Davy Crockett," the theme of a popular television program produced by Walt Disney.

His favorite class was wood shop, because the teacher would let him refinish his old guitars. However, many times he had to be reminded to quit playing and start working.

When he was still in junior high, Ritchie was a good enough musician to join some high school friends in a band called the Silhouettes. They played at dances and parties in the San Fernando Valley. When it was his turn to sing, he usually did Little Richard numbers. Sometimes he would perform a tune he had written himself, "Come On, Let's Go."

When he attended San Fernando High School, he met Donna Ludwig, a pretty blonde he would never forget. He also began playing regularly at school assemblies. "He would just tear up that assembly," Ludwig said. "They would holler and scream, jump up and down: I remember one assembly they wouldn't let him out! He had to keep on playing. The principal tried to call the assembly over and the kids wouldn't leave."[1]

Steve Valenzuela died when Ritchie was just ten, and the family never had much money. In January 1958, his mother, Connie, didn't have enough to make a $65 house payment. Ritchie saved the day by staging a dance at a local hall. He and the Silhouettes provided the music. By charging $1.25 per person, and $2 per couple, he raised $125.

One of the people at the dance was Doug Macchia. He taped the band, then told his friend Bob Keane about them. Keane had just started his own record company and was interested in rock and roll musicians. When he heard the tape, he set up an audition with Ritchie. It didn't take him long to sign the sixteen-year-old for his Del-Fi Records.

"Come On, Let's Go" was a song Valenzuela had been working on and singing since junior high school. It was a bouncy, fun tune that was very easy to dance to. In the summer of 1958, it became his first song to be released.

On the record label, his name had been shortened to Ritchie Valens. His real last name seemed too long for most fans to pronounce or remember. Because of the name change, most listeners never realized that Ritchie was Mexican-American, but Ritchie never tried to hide the fact that he was Chicano. His second release was "La Bamba," a catchy Spanish song from Mexico. He had heard it at family gatherings ever since he was a little boy. In certain parts of Mexico, it is still sung at weddings when the bride and groom dance.

Ritchie's Spanish was not good. In fact, he probably didn't even know what the song was about.[2] When he recorded it, Keane stood behind him, whispering the words.[3]

When "La Bamba" was released in October 1958, its flip side was "Donna." Even though Ritchie and Donna Ludwig never really dated, the singer thought about her a lot. When he finished writing the song, he sang it to her over the phone.

"Come On, Let's Go" was Valens's first Top Fifty hit. Less than a year later, he was dead at the age of seventeen.

Ritchie quit school to concentrate on his music career. He was on the road for weeks at a time performing with other young stars like Buddy Holly, the Big Bopper, and Dion and the Belmonts. When he came home to California, he liked to relax with his family and friends. He was irritated when some of the girls who had made fun of his weight tried to hang around him. "You treated me badly but now that I got it made you wanted to be my friend, but that ain't gonna work," he told them. "You can buy my records, but don't be my friend 'cause you ain't."[4]

On Halloween in 1958, he was staying with an aunt in California. When trick-or-treaters arrived, she realized she didn't have any candy in the house, so she told them, "I'll give you a treat. You can listen to Ritchie Valens."[5] The children threw their bags on the lawn and raced inside for a private concert.

On February 2, 1959, seventeen-year-old Ritchie Valens played his last concert at the Surf Ballroom in Clear Lake, Iowa. He was one of the big stars on the Winter Dance Party tour. Besides performing his own songs, he also joined Holly and the Big Bopper as a trio near the end of the show.

The next performance was scheduled for Moorehead, Minnesota, more than four hundred miles away. Holly decided he didn't want to ride the tour bus that far, so he chartered a small airplane. There was some discussion about who would get to ride on the plane. "Come on, let's flip a coin," Valens told a member of Holly's band. "Heads I go, tails you go."[6] The coin came up heads and Ritchie got on the plane just after midnight with Holly, the Big Bopper, and the pilot.

The tour bus arrived in Moorehead the next afternoon, but the plane crashed just eight miles from Clear Lake. Everybody on board was killed.

Ritchie Valens was dead, but, for a while, his records kept selling. "Donna" had been No. 2 in January; then it began to fade. After his death, it began to sell again and was No. 2 in March. At about the same time, his only completed album, *Ritchie Valens,* was released.

In the decades since the plane crash, his music has been recorded by a variety of performers. Some rock historians say that it was the wild, exciting guitar sound of "La Bamba" that inspired musicians twenty years later to create the punk rock sound.[7]

However, by the late 1970s, it was almost impossible to buy his original recordings. Ritchie Valens had been almost forgotten. It took the movie, *La Bamba,* released in 1987 with Lou Diamond Phillips starring as Valens, to bring attention to his music again. Los Lobos, a Chicano band from Los Angeles, performed his music for the movie. Their version of "La Bamba" was the nation's No. 1 song for three weeks in the summer of 1987.

It didn't really matter that the movie was a fictionalized account of his life. Much of the action portrayed never really happened. What was important was that millions of people were once again enjoying the music of a gifted performer and songwriter.

Suggested Recordings

In Concert at Pacoima Jr. High (Rhino, 1960)
Best of Ritchie Valens (Rhino, 1986)
Ritchie Valens Story (Rhino, 1993)

The Beach Boys (clockwise from top center, Brian Wilson, Carl Wilson, Mike Love, Al Jardine, and Dennis Wilson)

The Beach Boys
Good Vibrations

Music was always important for the Wilson brothers—Brian, Dennis, and Carl. On family trips, Dennis said, "We used to sing three-part harmony in the back of the car."[1] When Brian was just eleven months old, their parents heard him humming "Battle Hymn of the Republic." One of his fourth-grade school projects was a song about a lumberjack. He played it on a toy ukelele.

Brian, the first son of Murry and Audree Wilson, was born June 20, 1942. His brothers followed quickly—Dennis, on December 4, 1944, and Carl, on December 21, 1946. The family's home was in Hawthorne, California, near Los Angeles and the Pacific Ocean. A few miles away lived their cousin, Mike Love, who was born on March 15, 1941.

Luckily for the Wilson brothers and their cousin,

Dennis loved to surf. He paddled his surfboard out into the ocean, then stood up and rode the waves. "We got together because Dennis wanted us to write surf songs," Brian said. "We tried it and it worked."[2]

Brian, Dennis, Carl, and Mike formed a musical group with Brian's classmate Al Jardine, who was born September 3, 1942, in Lima, Ohio. At first they were Carl and the Passions, then Kenny and the Cadets, and The Pendletons, before settling on The Beach Boys.

One of the first songs Brian wrote was "Surfin'." He turned it in as a project for his high school music class, but the teacher gave him an F. That didn't stop the boys from recording the song on a local record label and releasing it in southern California. Soon they were recording for Capitol Records, a national company.

Brian kept writing surf songs. When he couldn't come up with an ending for "Surf City," he gave it to his friend Jan Berry, half of the group Jan and Dean. Berry finished the song, recorded it with Dean Torrence, and by July 1993, it was No. 1.

The Beach Boys recorded "Surfin' Safari," "Surfin' USA," and "Surfer Girl." Their music was happy and light, marked by their clear, beautiful harmonies, and their records were hits. At concerts, Mike explained how they produced their unique sound: "First we start with Denny on the drums. Then Al with the rhythm guitar. Then Carl with the lead guitar. Then Brian fills the instruments in with

The Beach Boys brought the sounds of California life to the rest of the country with vocal harmonies and smoothly blended guitars.

the bass."[3] Love usually sang lead. Even though Dennis was the only one who could surf, they were all pictured with surfboards on their album covers. In concert, they wore white jeans and blue-and-white-striped shirts.

Brian wanted the group to be more than just a surfing band. "In My Room," had nothing to do with waves or surfboards. It was a slow ballad, which he sang in falsetto, about a young man who needed time and a place to think. "I Get Around," their first No. 1 tune in 1963, was a rocker about a dissatisfied kid looking for action and excitement. However, most of their records continued to be good time music—"California Girls," "Little Deuce Coupe," "Be True to Your School," and "Fun, Fun, Fun."

Brian wasn't having much fun. He was tired of touring with the band, and he was embarrassed by the clothes they wore onstage. "I suddenly felt un-hip, as if we looked more like golf caddies than rock and roll stars."[4] He wanted more time to work on his music. After suffering a nervous breakdown in 1964, Brian quit touring with the band. He stayed at the studio to write songs that he recorded with the rest of the group when they weren't playing concerts. Onstage, he was eventually replaced by Bruce Johnston.

Capitol interrupted Brian's composing efforts by asking for another "fun" album, so they quickly recorded *Beach Boys Party!* Capitol claimed that all the music was recorded at a party at Love's house, but the "party" was really two sessions at the recording studio. Dean Torrence wandered into the session and sang lead on "Barbara Ann," the album's biggest hit. Since his contract prohibited him from recording with anybody but Jan and Dean, he never got credit for his efforts.

With *Beach Boys Party!* out of the way, Brian went back to work. When the band came back from the road, he was ready with many new songs and lots of new ideas. Instead of just guitars and drums, he wanted the music to include strings and a full orchestra. In fact, the rest of the band wouldn't even need to play instruments. All they would have to do was add their harmonies to the music Brian was putting together. Not everybody in the band liked his ideas. "Who's gonna hear this?" Love complained. "The ears of a dog?"[5] That gave Brian the idea for the album's title—*Pet Sounds.*

It took twenty-three musicians to back Carl's vocals on "God Only Knows." After an exhausting session, Brian was finally satisfied. He called the finished product "a rich, heavenly blanket of song."[6]

Another highlight of *Pet Sounds* was "Sloop John B," a folk-style song suggested by Jardine. Near the finish, something very unusual happens. The music stops and the group keeps singing a cappella. That was a common style for classical music, but very unusual for a rock song.

Brian wanted *Pet Sounds* to be as good—and as interesting—as the music being produced in England by the Beatles. Paul McCartney, who wrote most of the Beatles' music with John Lennon, was impressed. "It was *Pet Sounds* that blew me out of the water. I love the album so much."[7] He called "God Only Knows" "the best song that had ever been written."[8]

It took the Beach Boys seventeen separate recording sessions over six weeks to record their next single "Good Vibrations." Brian conducted the harpsichord, sleigh bells, organ, cello, and flutes that backed Carl's lead vocals. "We'd double or triple or quadruple the exact same part, so it would sound like twenty voices," Carl said, but he wasn't sure he liked the finished product.[9] "Boy," he said, "that's really bizarre sounding music."[10] "Good Vibrations" might have sounded bizarre, but it was very popular, hitting No. 1 in December 1966.

Right away Brian went to work on an album he hoped would go beyond *Pet Sounds*. For months, he worked on tracks for *Smile*, but his drug abuse and depression made it extremely difficult. "Brian ran into all sorts of problems on *Smile*," Carl said. He just couldn't find the right direction to finish it."[11] When he gave up, Brian destroyed many of the master tapes, and the album was lost.

Over the next twenty years, the Beach Boys continued to release new music, but it was usually ignored. Their fans wanted to hear the group's simple, happy early songs. *Endless Summer,* a collection of their greatest hits, was a No. 1 album in 1974. The band began concentrating its attention on concerts. For more than a hundred days a year, they were on the road.

Their Fourth of July concerts near the Washington Monument in Washington, D.C., were an annual event until Interior Secretary James Watt canceled their appearance in 1982. When he said the Beach Boys attracted the "wrong element" to the capital, fans across the country came to their defense. One of them was President Ronald Reagan, who invited the group to the White House.

After the 1960s, the Beach Boys had only two big singles. "Rock and Roll Music," a remake of the classic Chuck Berry tune, rose to No. 5 in 1976. In 1988, they were given a chance to work on the soundtrack for *Cocktail,* a Tom Cruise movie about a bartender. Love wrote "Kokomo" with three other musicians and sang lead. Using steel drums and congas, he said, "We flavored it like a tropical breeze."[12] It was No. 1 in November of 1988.

After apparently putting most of his substance abuse and mental problems behind him, Brian worked hard to get back in shape, lost a hundred pounds, and occasionally returned to the stage. In recent years, because of legal and musical disagreements with the rest of the group, his appearances with them have become very rare. He wasn't in the studio when "Kokomo" was recorded, but he released his first solo album the same year.

For years, Dennis had also struggled with drug and alcohol abuse. Late in 1983, after a day of drinking, he dove off a marina into the Pacific Ocean and drowned.

Despite his death and the continuing arguments with Brian, the other Beach Boys have continued to tour. "The Beach Boys' version of rock and roll has always been fun," Love said. "Our friends know that a Beach Boys concert was like a celebration of summer, good times, and friends."[13]

Suggested Recordings

Beach Boys Today! (Capitol, 1965)
Summer Days (And Summer Nights!)
(Capitol, 1965)
Pet Sounds (Capitol, 1966)
Smiley Smile (Capitol, 1967)
Surf's Up (Caribou, 1971)
Endless Summer (Capitol, 1974)
Absolute Best, Vol. 1 (Capitol, 1991)
Absolute Best, Vol. 2 (Capitol, 1991)
Good Vibrations: Thirty Years of the Beach Boys
(Capitol, 1993)

Bob Dylan

6

Bob Dylan

The Times They Are A-Changin'

"I always wanted to be a guitar player and a singer," Bob Dylan said after he became a star. "Since I was ten, eleven or twelve, it was all that interested me. That was the only thing that I did that meant anything really."[1]

In the 1950s, when he was still Bobby Zimmerman growing up in Hibbing, Minnesota, country music was what he enjoyed and played. His favorite performer was Hank Williams.

His father, Abraham Zimmerman, was an appliance dealer, and the family had plenty of money. Sometimes Bobby helped his dad deliver washing machines and refrigerators. He also went with him to homes where poor families had difficulty paying their appliance bills. Mr. Zimmerman wanted his son to know that, for many people, life wasn't easy.

By the time he was fifteen, Bob had begun to enjoy rock and roll music. Even though he was usually a quiet, shy person, he decided he wanted to be a performer, so he joined a band called the Shadow Blasters. In 1956, they auditioned for a show in Hibbing, singing Little Richard's "Long Tall Sally." With the loud guitar music, nobody could hear Bob's singing. The Shadow Blasters didn't get the job.

His next band, the Golden Chords, had better luck. They played regularly in restaurants and talent shows. "He would get up and do songs, imitating Elvis and so on, and it was hilarious! To hear this wild singing coming out of a boy who kept to himself, [who] was really very quiet," said a friend.[2] He also played with the Satin Tones, and with Elston Gunn and the Rock Boppers.

Mr. Zimmerman thought rock and roll music was a waste of time. Why couldn't Bob get a real job? Why couldn't he dress up? Why did he always have to wear sunglasses and jeans? Why couldn't he get a decent haircut? But Bob wasn't interested in changing. Finally, after his son graduated from Hibbing High School in 1959, Mr. Zimmerman sent him to a school in Pennsylvania that specialized in dealing with rebellious teenagers.

The school didn't change Bob, either. He soon left Pennsylvania to enroll at the University of Minnesota in Minneapolis. Not surprisingly, he was much more interested in his music than in attending classes. By then, he was usually playing folk music, instead of rock and roll. Now he didn't need a band. He could accompany himself on his acoustic guitar. When he auditioned at the Ten O'Clock Scholar coffeehouse in Minneapolis, he told the owner his name was Bob Dylan. He later said the name just came to him. He took it from Dylan Thomas, a Welsh poet then popular with many young people.

In the summer of 1960, Dylan hitchhiked to Denver with his guitar. He couldn't find much work there, but learned to play the harmonica from the folksinger Jesse Fuller, who wore the instrument in a brace around his neck. Dylan was intrigued by the idea of being able to play the harmonica without letting go of his guitar. The instrument would give his music a new sound.

At about the same time, he read *Bound for Glory,* Woody Guthrie's autobiography. During the Great Depression, Guthrie had begun his career as a folksinger, telling the stories of poor families struggling to survive. Dylan had a new musical hero.

When he returned to Minnesota, he was imitating Guthrie's style in music, clothing, and speaking. "He came back talking with a real thick Oklahoma accent and wearing a cowboy hat and boots," said his friend Bonnie Beecher. "He was into Woody Guthrie in a big, big way."[3]

After a few months in Minneapolis, Dylan decided to move to New York City. He hoped there would be more people there who would enjoy his music. He would also be close to the hospital in New Jersey where Guthrie was slowly dying from Huntington's disease.

Dylan's fame began to spread almost as soon as he moved into the Greenwich Village section of New York City. He performed at popular coffeehouses. He played the harmonica on recordings by stars like Harry Belafonte, then signed a recording contract of his own with Columbia Records. He became good friends with Joan Baez, the country's most popular folksinger. He paid regular visits to Guthrie's hospital room.

Not everybody liked his voice. They said it was scratchy, nasal, and irritating. Sometimes, they thought, it sounded like he was whining or howling, not really singing. However, his fans thought his voice was moving and unique because it showed so much feeling.

At first he sang songs by Guthrie and other folksingers. Then he began using more and more of his own compositions. Soon other groups were performing his material. Dylan first became well known when Peter, Paul and Mary recorded his song "Blowin' in the Wind." It was a pretty song, but it made people think, too. Dylan wanted people to think about love, death, and war. In the early 1960s, most popular songs had simple, even silly lyrics. Records like "Alley-Oop" and "Itsy Bitsy Teenie Weenie Yellow Polka Dot Bikini" didn't require listeners to do much thinking. Dylan's songs were different. The lyrics were at least as important as the melodies.

"Masters of War" was an angry song that attacked politicians, generals, and corporate executives who profited from the deaths of people in war. "I did what I could while I was there . . . in the struggle for peoples' freedom, individual or otherwise," Dylan said. "I hate oppression, especially on children."[4]

"The Times They Are A-Changin'" foreshadowed the rebellion of the hippies and student radicals in the late 1960s. "I wanted to write a big song, some kind of theme song, ya know, with short concise verses that piled up on each other in a hypnotic way."[5]

"Like a Rolling Stone," in 1965, was the first big hit he sang himself. It began with a riff he borrowed from Ritchie Valens's "La Bamba." Between the verses, he injected some intense harmonica playing. The song is an attack on pretentious people who feel they're better than everybody else. It was one of his first real rock and roll songs.

For the past thirty years, Dylan has continued to irritate his critics and surprise his fans. He's not interested in giving people what they expect—or want. When he was booked on *The Ed Sullivan Show*, the most popular television variety program in the 1960s, the producers tried to tell him which of his songs he could sing. They didn't want their viewers to be upset by his protest music. Dylan left the studio and never appeared on the show. When

Bob Dylan blended country, folk, blues, and poetry to create what is now known as "folk rock."

he first appeared in public with an electric, not an accoustic, guitar, the crowd booed him off the stage. In the late 1970s when he began singing about becoming a Christian, many fans complained that he sounded like a second-rate preacher. When he is not in the mood for a show, he mumbles the lyrics or leaves the stage after only a few songs.

Dylan has even attacked his own music. "The world don't need any more songs. If nobody wrote any songs from this day on, the world ain't gonna suffer for it."[6] What about all the great material he has written? "If you see me do it, any idiot can do it."[7]

By now, Dylan's fans have learned to ignore his occasionally strange behavior and just concentrate on his songs. He continues to record new music and appear in concerts. Fans remember that he had the courage to sing at the March on Washington in 1963 when Martin Luther King, Jr. delivered his "I Have a Dream" speech. In 1971, he helped earn millions for hunger relief at the Concert for Bangla Desh in New York City. Backed by Keith Richards and Ron Wood, of the Rolling Stones, he was the closing act at the massive Live Aid benefit to raise money for the victims of an African famine in 1985.

In the 1980s, Dylan demonstrated that he still had a sense of humor when he pretended to be Lucky Wilbury, part of a band of brothers on the album *Volume One* by the Traveling Wilburys. His "brothers" were Lefty (the late Roy Orbison, who recorded "Pretty Woman" in the 1960s), Nelson (George Harrison of the Beatles), Otis (Jeff Lynne of Electric Light Orchestra), and Charlie T. Jr. (Tom Petty, of Tom Petty and the Heartbreakers). The idea of a mythical band of brothers was silly, most critics agreed, but a good excuse to bring together some great musicians.

Today Bob Dylan remains one of the world's most respected songwriters and performers. In 1988, he was inducted into the Rock and Roll Hall of Fame. "Dylan was a revolutionary," Bruce Springsteen said. "Bob freed your mind the way Elvis freed your body. . . . He invented a new way a pop singer could sound . . . and changed the face of rock and roll forever."[8]

Suggested Recordings

Freewheelin' Bob Dylan (Columbia, 1963)
Times They Are A-Changin' (Columbia, 1964)
Another Side of Bob Dylan (Columbia, 1964)
Bring It All Back Home (Columbia, 1965)
Highway 61 Revisited (Columbia, 1965)
Blonde on Blonde (Columbia, 1966)
John Wesley Harding (Columbia, 1968)
Nashville Skyline (Columbia, 1969)
Bob Dylan's Greatest Hits, Vol. 2
(Columbia, 1971)
Blood on the Tracks (Columbia, 1975)
Basement Tapes (Columbia, 1975)
Desire (Columbia, 1976)
Biograph (Columbia, 1985)

Aretha Franklin

Aretha Franklin
The Queen of Soul

When she was a little girl, Aretha Franklin watched Clara Ward, a great gospel star, perform "Peace in the Valley." Most performers would have sung it slowly and solemnly, but not Ward. She tore off her hat, threw it to the floor, and belted out the song at the top of her lungs. Aretha loved the intense feeling Ward poured into the spiritual. "That," she said, "was when I wanted to be a singer."[1]

Aretha was born on March 25, 1943, in Buffalo, New York, but moved to Detroit, Michigan, when she was two. Her father, the Reverend C. L. Franklin, was pastor of New Bethel Baptist Church, one of Detroit's largest black congregations. He preached the way Aretha wanted to sing. He swayed, trembled, screamed, and whispered his way through his sermons. Reverend Franklin was an exciting, inspirational man. It wasn't unusual for people to faint during his services.

When she was twelve, Aretha stepped out of the choir to sing solos at her father's church. Her voice was strong, full, and beautiful. Just like her father, she seemed to shake the walls.

Several months a year, Reverend Franklin spoke at religious revivals across the country. When Aretha was just fourteen, she joined the tours as a singer. The worshippers loved the way she ripped into the spirituals. Some of her performances were recorded and released on the album *Songs of Faith*. It sold thousands of copies, mostly to the same people who bought records of her father's sermons. Aretha looked like she was on her way to becoming a star.

But then she got pregnant. She was only fifteen when her son, Clarence Franklin, was born in 1957. She quit high school and gave up performing to take care of the baby, but she continued to listen to records and pound out music of her own on the piano. She also watched popular singers like Dinah Washington perform when they came to Detroit. She became interested in blues music and jazz as well as gospel music.

After three years, Aretha decided she wasn't cut out to be a full-time, stay-at-home mother. Music was her life. She had to perform. She wanted a career as a singer. In 1960, she left her son with her family and moved to New York City.

Friends quickly arranged an audition with John

Hammond of Columbia Records. He was the man who had discovered Billie Holiday, the great blues singer, thirty years before. Later he would sign such stars as Bob Dylan and Bruce Springsteen. In 1960, he signed Aretha Franklin.

She was just eighteen years old and seemed to be just a few hit records away from becoming a star, but the big hits never came with Columbia Records. The company arranged for her to sing in clubs, but she missed the backing of a choir and the attention of her listeners. The crowds in the clubs were eating, drinking, and talking. "I was afraid," she said. "I sang to the floor a lot."[2] On her records, the Columbia executives had her sing slow jazz songs, some quiet rhythm and blues, and other bland tunes. They didn't let her pour her heart and soul into the music. "It wasn't really me," she said.[3]

In 1966, Aretha's contract with Columbia expired. Her records had sold so poorly that she owed the company some money, but she was signed very quickly by Jerry Wexler, vice president of Atlantic Records. "She's a musical genius," he said.[4]

Right away Wexler and Aretha went to work at making her a star. She left New York for a recording studio in Muscle Shoals, Alabama. "We've got these rhythm sections down south," he said, "and I've got a hunch that . . . she's not singing as well as when she was singing gospel songs."[5] At the one-day session, Aretha recorded "I Never Loved a Man (The Way I Loved You)," and Wexler knew his hunch was right. Her voice sailed effortlessly from the tune's low notes to its soaring high ones. That short song had more emotion and excitement than all of the albums she had recorded in New York. It sold a million copies.

While Aretha was hot, Atlantic wanted to cut an album. This time she was joined in New York by the rhythm section from Muscle Shoals. They finished the album in just a week. "She'd sit down at the piano, play a song," said recording engineer Tom Dowd. "We were doing Aretha in gospel/blues tradition, unlike the elegant production things she had been doing at Columbia."[6]

One of the songs chosen for the session was "Respect," written and originally sung by Otis Redding. It was a simple song, demanding respect from a woman when her husband gets home from a hard day. "Respect" seemed like an odd selection for a young woman to sing, but Aretha worked to make it her own. "She had a piano at home," Wexler said, "and she would sit there with her sisters."[7] Aretha and her sister, Carolyn, decided to spell out the word "R-E-S-P-E-C-T" in the middle of the song. They also added the repeated line, "Sock it to me!"

"When she started singing, all the parts became obvious—and it was just 'Boom, here it is,'" Dowd said.[8] It was a wild, exciting performance as Aretha screamed and pleaded. The meaning of the song had changed completely. Now it was about a woman with an attitude who demanded—and deserved—some

The Queen of Soul has had more million-selling albums than any other woman in recording history.

"respect" from her man. "I just lost my song," Redding said. "That girl took it away from me."[9]

"Respect" was a monster hit. It was Aretha's first No. 1 song. Suddenly she was one of the hottest singers in show business. Fans began calling her the Queen of Soul.

At a concert in Georgia, she was concentrating so hard on her music that she didn't notice she was too close to the edge of the stage. When she fell off, she shattered her right elbow. Even that didn't slow her down. She headed into the studio with a cast to record her second album, *Aretha Arrives.* Against her doctor's orders, she played the piano on many of the songs. The music on "You Are My Sunshine" was so fast that she had to give her right arm a rest while she played the whole thing with her left hand.

On February 16, 1968, she returned in triumph to Detroit for Aretha Franklin Day. She was cheered by twelve thousand fans at Cobo Hall as she sang all her hits and then received Female Vocalist of the Year awards from three music magazines: *Billboard, Cash Box,* and *Record World.* Dr. Martin Luther King, Jr., was there to present her an award from the Southern Christian Leadership Council. It was a very special evening for the superstar. "Dr. King was a wonderful, wonderful, fine man as well as a civil rights leader," she said. "He and my dad were great friends."[10] After King's death seven weeks later, she sang "Precious Lord" at his funeral in Atlanta.

In the late 1960s, she continued turning out

classic music—"(You Make Me Feel Like) A Natural Woman," "Chain of Fools," and "The House That Jack Built." She even had success with a couple of slow ballads, "I Say a Little Prayer" and the Beatles' "Eleanor Rigby."

Franklin's power as a performer was captured on the classic album *Aretha Live at Fillmore West,* released in 1971. From her explosive entrance with "Respect" through a wild encore with Ray Charles on "Spirit in the Dark," the cheering crowd is hers.

In 1980, she appeared in *The Blues Brothers,* her first movie. It tells the story of Jake and Elwood Blues (John Belushi and Dan Aykroyd) and their efforts to put together a blues band. When they try to talk one of the musicians into joining them, he has to face his wife, played by Franklin, the owner of a soul food restaurant. Dressed in a dirty waitress's uniform, Aretha breaks into the song "Think." It's an intimidating performance. She was perfect in the role of a woman without time or patience for a man who wanted to cut out with his friends.

Some of Franklin's best music in the 1980s was recorded with other artists. She sang, "Sisters Are Doin' It for Themselves," a feminist anthem, with Annie Lennox of the Eurythmics. George Michael flew to Detroit to record "I Knew You Were Waiting (For Me)." Narada Michael Walden, the record's producer, said, "It was really a memorable moment. And fortunately . . . a lot of that magic is in that record. . . . They worked side by side kicking each other and just pushing it and made it happen."[11] The song was No. 1 in April 1987, almost twenty years after "Respect." That same year she became the first woman inducted into the Rock and Roll Hall of Fame.

Today Franklin is still a giant in the music world. She continues to record and perform, and her influence is reflected in the music of a new generation of singers who grew up listening to her. Whitney Houston's mother, Cissy, has been singing background vocals for Aretha for more than thirty years. "I remember when I was six or seven, crawling up to the window to watch my mother sing," Whitney said. "And I'd be talking to Aunt Ree. I had no idea that Aretha Franklin was famous—just that I liked to hear her sing, too!" Houston loved the way Aunt Ree sang. "It came from deep down within. That's what I want to do."[12]

Aretha also gave a break to Oprah Winfrey, the actress and talk show host. In 1968, Winfrey was a homeless fourteen-year-old in Chicago when she saw Franklin's limousine pull up to a hotel. "I ran up to her crying my eyes out . . . By the time we reached the front door of the hotel, she pulled one hundred dollars out of her purse and gave it to me."[13]

Times have changed for Oprah. By the 1990s, she was earning more money than any other woman in show business. Not much has changed for Aretha. She's still thrilling people with her magnificent voice.

Suggested Recordings

I Never Loved A Man (The Way I Love You)
(Atlantic, 1967)
Lady Soul (Atlantic, 1967)
Aretha Now (Atlantic, 1968)
Spirit in the Dark (Atlantic, 1970)
Sparkle (Rhino, 1976)
30 Greatest Hits (Atlantic, 1986)
Queen of Soul: The Atlantic Recordings
(Rhino, 1992)

The Doors (left to right, Jim Morrison, John Densmore, Ray Manzarek, and Robby Krieger)

8

The Doors

Strange Days

Jim Morrison was a college student in 1964 when he came up with a name for his band. He was inspired by Aldous Huxley's book *The Doors of Perception*. He also liked a mysterious sentence written by William Blake: "There are things that are known and things that are unknown, in between the doors."[1] The band would be the Doors.

When Morrison came up with the name he didn't even have a band. Someday, though, he hoped to put one together. In the meantime, he would continue to write poetry and attend classes at UCLA's film school in Los Angeles.

By the time he was attending college in California, Morrison had lived in many cities across the United States. His father, Steve, was a Navy officer, who married his wife, Clara, just before his ship was sent to the Pacific early in World War II. Their first son, James Douglas, was born December 8, 1943, in Pensacola, Florida.

Ray Daniel Manzarek was born February 12, 1939, in Chicago, Illinois. His parents had forced him to take piano lessons when he was growing up. He hated the instrument until he discovered boogie-woogie and blues. After studying classical music at the Chicago Conservatory, he, too, enrolled at UCLA. In the summer of 1965, he met Morrison on the beach in Venice, California. His friend sang him "Moonlight Drive," a song he had just written. Manzarek was astonished. "I'd never heard lyrics to a rock song like that before. We talked awhile before we decided to get a group together and make a million dollars."[2] Of course, the group already had a name.

Morrison would sing and Manzarek would play piano, organ, and flute. A rock band needs guitars and drums, too, so Manzarek brought his friends John Densmore and Robbie Krieger into the group. Densmore, born December 1, 1944, in Santa Monica, California, was a veteran drummer, usually in jazz bands. After being born on January 8, 1946, in Los Angeles, Krieger had grown up in a home filled with the sounds of classical music and the marches his parents loved. After learning to play the piano and trumpet, he switched to the guitar when he was seventeen.

Morrison and his bandmates wanted a bass player

to round out their sound, but they couldn't find anybody they felt was good enough. They finally quit looking when Manzarek discovered a new electronic keyboard that sounded like a bass and an organ. He could produce the sounds of both instruments at once.

The Doors earned twenty dollars a night playing at a small club called London Fog. By this time, Morrison had only written a few songs, so they had to perform music already recorded by others. Playing four sets a night, seven days a week, the group had a chance to develop a unique sound. Manzarek's keyboard made them different from most rock bands, which relied solely on guitars and drums, but their lead singer was what really set them apart. At first, Morrison seemed shy and uncomfortable onstage, but, as he gained confidence, he became louder and wilder. He grew accustomed to being the center of attention—and he enjoyed it. Sometimes he interrupted the songs to recite poetry or just to ramble on about nearly anything. Sometimes he didn't make much sense, but the audiences couldn't take their eyes off him. He was a strikingly handsome man who almost looked too young to be up so late at a club. His voice, of course, was his biggest asset. It was intense and strong, filled with the emotion of the music.

Morrison continued to write interesting songs. One of his strangest was "The End," a slow, solemn statement about violence and death. It was performed at the Whiskey-A-Go-Go, one of the most important clubs in Los Angeles. At the end of the eleven-minute song, the fascinated crowd was too stunned to applaud or even speak, but the club's manager had heard enough. "Those guys are nuts!" he yelled. "Get them out of here."[3]

But the Doors didn't need the Whiskey-A-Go-Go any more. Late in 1966, they recorded their first album for Elektra Records. Their producer, Paul A. Rothchild, loved "The End." "I don't know if you know what's happening here," he told his engineer during the session, "but magic is being made. We are recording magic."[4]

Morrison suggested that the other members of the group write some songs to go with his. "In order to compete with Jim's songs," said Krieger, "I knew I'd have to be pretty good."[5] Since he liked the Rolling Stones' "Play With Fire," he decided to write about fire, too. Manzarek helped out by suggesting the catchy keyboard introduction, and Densmore came up with the beat. Morrison wrote some of the lyrics in the second verse. When they were finished, "Light My Fire" was almost seven minutes long. It was a great song, but Elektra executives were afraid it was so long that radio stations wouldn't play it. They left the long version on the album, but shortened the single release by cutting out a long instrumental section in the middle.

During the summer of 1967, "Light My Fire" was the No. 1 song in the United States for three weeks. The album, *The Doors*, sold more than a million copies. Their second album, *Strange Days*, had two more single hits, "People Are Strange" and "Love Me Two Times."

Morrison was not an easy man to work with. During his years at UCLA, he experimented with LSD, a powerful hallucinogenic drug. By the time the Doors had hit the big time, he had gone from drugs to alcohol. Sometimes he was so drunk he didn't show up for concerts or recording sessions. When he did show, he wasn't always in good enough shape to sing. Strangely enough, Morrison's problems with alcohol and his undependability seemed to make him even more popular with his young fans. They thought of him as a fun-loving rebel who wouldn't let authorities order him around. He said and did outrageous things. "I've always been attracted to ideas that were about revolt against authority," he announced. "I am interested in anything about revolt, disorder, chaos—especially activity that seems to have no meaning."[6] Many adults thought he was weird and dangerous. They banned some of the band's songs from the radio and prevented them from performing in several cities.

When the Doors began working on their third album, Morrison was usually too drunk to record. At one session, Densmore threw his drumsticks across the studio and threatened to quit the band. While they waited for their lead singer to sober up, the rest of the band read a stack of poems he had

Morrison's dramatic onstage performances at the Whiskey-A-Go-Go
helped earn the Doors a record deal with Elektra.

written three years before. One of them was "Hello, I Love You," a tribute to a beautiful girl he had watched walking along a beach. Morrison had music to go with the words, and he was eventually able to record it. "Hello, I Love You" reached No. 1 in August of 1968.

"The Unknown Soldier" was a passionate antiwar song recorded for the same album. At one point, the music stops for the sounds of a firing squad killing a soldier. Onstage, Morrison collapsed when Densmore faked the sound of a gun shot by breaking a drumstick on the rim of a drum. Coming at the height of the Vietnam War, "The Unknown Soldier" caused more controversy. Morrison produced one of the earliest music videos to go along with the song. He also wrote volumes of poetry while the group waited for him to work on the new album.

Waiting for the Sun was finally completed, and the Doors began touring again. By then, Morrison was almost totally out of control. One of his favorite tricks was belching into the microphone. Many of his fans began to lose patience, and sometimes he was booed. They wanted to hear him sing, not belch and blabber as he wandered the stage in a drunken stupor.

In Phoenix, he made obscene gestures and swore at the audience. He threatened to "get" Richard Nixon, the newly elected president, and then invited the crowd to come to the stage. In Queens, New York, he ended the concert by falling on his back and screaming. The audience responded by breaking chairs and charging onstage. In Amsterdam, Holland, he collapsed and was rushed to the hospital. Manzarek, Krieger, and Densmore did the concert without him, taking turns singing. In a Miami auditorium, Morrison screamed obscenities, slugged concert officials, and undressed on stage. For that, he was arrested and convicted of indecent exposure and profanity.

Soon after the trial, he decided to go to France to rest and write. Just before he left, he tried to swing into his hotel window by jumping off a second-story roof and grabbing a rain gutter. When his hand slipped, he fell to the ground, but he wasn't seriously injured. "I'm like a cat, you know, the nine-lives trip?" he told a friend. "That's me." He figured the fall had used up his eighth life. "The point I'm trying to make is, I might not ever come back from Paris. . . . And if I don't, then you'll know the cat's run outta lives."[7]

Once in France, he wrote—and ate and drank. By then, he was overweight and complaining of chest pains. On July 3, 1971, the twenty-seven-year-old singer died of a heart attack in Paris.

In the years since Morrison's death, the group's music has remained popular. *The Doors,* a movie released in 1991 starring Val Kilmer, introduced them to a whole new generation of fans. Jim Morrison's music and attitude have made him a hero to teenagers who weren't even born when he died.

Suggested Recordings

Waiting for the Sun (Elektra, 1968)
Morrison Hotel (Hard Rock Cafe)
(Elektra, 1970)
L.A. Woman (Elektra, 1971)
Weird Scenes Inside the Gold Mine
(Elektra, 1972)
Best of the Doors (Elektra, 1974)

Jimi Hendrix

9

Jimi Hendrix
Purple Haze

Johnny Hendrix didn't meet his father until he was almost three years old. When the boy was born on November 27, 1942, in Seattle, Washington, Al Hendrix was serving in the army. Johnny stayed first with his mother, Lucille, then with family friends in California.

After World War II ended in 1945, Al Hendrix came home, divorced his wife and took his son to Seattle. Soon, he changed the boy's name from John Allen to James Marshall.

Jimmy was a shy child who loved music. "My first instrument was a harmonica, when I was about four," he said. "Next, though, it was a violin. I always loved string instruments and pianos, then I started digging guitars."[1]

Muddy Waters was the first guitarist whose music

he remembered: "I heard one of his records when I was a little boy and it scared me to death because I heard all these *sounds*. It was great."[2]

In high school, he and his friends formed a band called the Rocking Kings. They played blues, and rock and roll, in halls around Seattle. At their first paying gig at a National Guard Armory, each member of the band earned thirty-five cents.

Hendrix quit school before graduating so he could join the army. He became part of the Screaming Eagles paratrooper squad that trained in Fort Campbell, Kentucky. After twenty-five successful parachute jumps, he broke his ankle on his twenty-sixth. That injury led to an honorable discharge after just thirteen months of service.

While in the army, Hendrix formed the King Kasuals, a rhythm and blues group, with bassist Billy Cox, another serviceman. They played at clubs in Kentucky and Tennessee. After his discharge, the band was still active until Jimmy went to New York, where he won $25 in an amateur contest at Harlem's Apollo Theatre. Soon he was working as a backup musician for such big-name acts as Sam Cooke, Jackie Wilson, the Isley Brothers, and Little Richard.

Hendrix then formed his own bands with names like Rain Flower, and Jimmy James and the Blue Flames. While playing small clubs in Greenwich Village, he was spotted by Chas Chandler, bassist for the Animals, a British rock group. Chandler offered to take Jimmy to London, manage his career, and get him a recording contract. Soon Al Hendrix, back in Seattle, got a message from his son: "It's me, Dad. I'm in England. I've met some people and they're going to make me a big star. We changed my name to J-I-M-I."[3]

Within a week after arriving in London, Jimi had a three-man band called the Jimi Hendrix Experience. Mitch Mitchell was the drummer and Noel Redding played bass guitar. Their concerts in France and England soon began to attract a good deal of attention—from fans as well as from stars like Eric Clapton and Paul McCartney. Of course, Hendrix was hard not to notice. He loved the colorful psychedelic style then popular, so he wore bright bell-bottom pants and wild flowered shirts and scarves. He was also one of the first black rock musicians who didn't cut his hair very short or process it so it was smooth. Instead, he had a huge, wavy Afro.

Jimi wasn't becoming famous because of his clothes or hair, though. It was his guitar playing that amazed his audiences. Even though he was left-handed, he played a right-handed guitar upside-down.[4] "He had these huge hands," said Mitchell. "His thumbs were nearly as long as his fingers. Like many blues players he could use it to his advantage hooking it over the neck of his guitar as an extra finger."[5]

Hendrix didn't just play the guitar; he attacked it. Many guitarists before him had used distortion and feedback, but he was the first to harness these strange effects and make them sound exactly the way

In 1966, bassist Noel Redding (with glasses) and drummer Mitch Mitchell joined Jimi Hendrix to form the Jimi Hendrix Experience.

he wanted them to sound. His guitar screeched and squealed, and he always played it very loudly.

Mike Bloomfield, a guitarist with the Paul Butterfield Blues Band, remembered the first time he saw Hendrix play: "In front of my eyes, he burned me to death. . . . H-bombs were going off, guided missiles were flying—I can't tell you the sounds he was getting out of his instrument. . . . How he did this, I wish I understood. He just got right up in my face with that axe [guitar]."[6]

In 1966, the Experience played a ferocious set at the Monterey Pop Festival. When he finished his final song, "Wild Thing," Hendrix sprayed his guitar with lighter fluid, knelt on the stage, and set the guitar on fire.

The Experience was booked as the opening act for the Monkees, a popular group with their own television show. As soon as Jimi hit the stage, the crowd began screaming, "We want the Monkees!" When he turned up the volume to catch their attention, they began to boo. "Eight-year-old kids with their mums and dads, no wonder they hated us," Mitchell said.[7] The band and the promoters agreed that the Experience and the Monkees were a terrible combination. To get them off the tour, Chandler explained, "I had to tell all these lies that [the Daughters of the American Revolution thought that] Hendrix was too outrageous and obscene."[8]

In the studio for their first album, *Are You Experienced?*, Jimi was hard on Redding and Mitchell.

He told them exactly how he wanted their instruments to sound. If they didn't get it right, he played the instruments himself.

Hendrix thought his singing voice was weak, but he respected Bob Dylan as a writer and a performer. Early in his career he reasoned that if Dylan's unusual voice was good enough for singing, so was his.[9] While recording *Are You Experienced?*, he was still so uncomfortable that the album's engineer built a small booth in the studio so nobody could watch him sing. At the end of each song, he'd poke his head out and ask, "Is that all right?"[10]

"Purple Haze," one of the band's first hits, featured Jimi's trademark guitar distortion and some very strange lyrics. What was the song about? "I had this thing on my mind about a dream I had that I was walking under the sea," he explained. "It's linked to a story I read in a science fiction magazine about a purple death ray."[11]

Hendrix didn't want to be known just for being some kind of psychedelic wild man. "He desperately wanted to expand his musical horizons," said Eddie Kramer, his recording engineer.[12] That's why he recorded Dylan's song "All Along the Watchtower." He took the folk song and "electrified" it with his guitar. Dylan was impressed. He later copied Hendrix's version when he played the song in concert.

Sometimes Jimi's antics onstage didn't help make people believe he was a serious musician. He liked to play the guitar behind his back and with his teeth. If he didn't burn it at the end of a show, he sometimes smashed it against his amplifiers. When he thought the crowd was satisfied by his flamboyant behavior, he didn't always attempt to play as well as he could.

Hendrix was the closing act at Woodstock, the legendary 1969 rock festival. By the time he played, it was morning and most of the fans had left. "It was so cold and damp at that time of the morning that none of our numbers really jelled," Mitchell said. "We just wanted to go home."[13] Without warning the band, Hendrix broke into "The Star-Spangled Banner." His guitar made the sounds of bombs exploding and planes screeching through the sky. Without singing a word, he turned the national anthem into a song of anger and anguish. Some people figured his performance was a protest against the Vietnam War, but Hendrix didn't talk much about politics. "I'm American so I played it," he said. "They made me sing it in school . . . I thought it was beautiful."[14]

Jimi's career came to a grotesque, tragic end when he was only twenty-seven years old. For years, he had abused drugs. On September 18, 1970, he took too many pills before sleeping, then choked to death on his own vomit.

He left behind almost a thousand hours of unreleased recorded music.[15] In the years since his death, a steady stream of it has been released. His original albums and collections of his greatest hits sell millions of copies every year. Hendrix probably would have been amused by his continuing popularity. "It's funny the way most people love the dead," he said. "Once you have died, you are made for life. You have to die before they think you are worth anything."[16]

Suggested Recordings

Are You Experienced? (Reprise, 1967)
Axis: Bold as Love (Reprise, 1967)
Smash Hits (Reprise, 1968)
Electric Ladyland (Reprise, 1968)
Band of Gypsies (Capitol, 1970)
Live at Winterland (Rykodisc, 1987)
Radio One (Rykodisc, 1989)

Bruce Springsteen

Bruce Springsteen

The Boss

Growing up in Freehold, New Jersey, where he was born on September 23, 1949, Bruce Frederick Joseph Springsteen was not a happy kid. "I didn't like school," he said. "I didn't like people."[1] The teachers didn't like him much, either. At St. Rose of Lima Grade School, one of them made him sit in a trash can under her desk. That was the only way she could get him to behave.[2]

The only thing he enjoyed was rock and roll music: "The radio in the fifties for me was miraculous. It was like TNT coming out of those speakers. It came in and grabbed you by the heart and lifted you up."[3]

Music even gave him his first hero: "Man, when I was nine, I couldn't imagine anyone not wanting to be Elvis Presley."[4] He convinced his mother to buy him a guitar, but his fingers weren't big enough to finger the strings.

"I was dead until I was thirteen," he said.[5] That was when he saved up $18, enough to buy a second-hand guitar that fit his fingers. After six months of practice, he joined his first band, the Rogues. For a year, they played at clubs and school dances. Bruce wasn't the group's lead singer, but he got to play the guitar, and he was happy. When the Rogues broke up, he joined the Castiles. They were paid $35 for their first professional gig at the Woodhaven Swim Club. For the first time, he began writing songs. At about the time he graduated from Freehold Regional High School in 1967, the Castiles broke up, too.

Springsteen kept playing, in groups named Earth, Steel Mill, and the Bruce Springsteen Band. In 1972, he decided to go it alone. He was out of money, and he realized he could never support himself playing in small-town bars and clubs in New Jersey. If he didn't hit the big time soon, he would have to give up music and find a regular job. His agent pestered record executive John Hammond until he agreed to give Bruce a brief audition. Two songs were all it took. Hammond told Springsteen, "You gotta be on Columbia records."[6] The next day Bruce recorded fourteen songs in the Columbia studio. As soon as the contract was signed, he lined up a new group of musicians, the E Street Band, to back him up on recordings and in concerts.

Springsteen's first two albums, *Greetings from*

Asbury Park, N.J., and *The Wild, the Innocent and the E Street Shuffle,* weren't big hits. Most of the songs were rockers that told the stories of the working-class people he had grown up with in New Jersey. He and the E Street Band played hundreds of concerts along America's East Coast. Their wild three-hour shows began building a following even among fans who had never heard their albums.

Bruce got his big break when Jon Landau, a prominent rock critic, reviewed a concert. "I saw rock 'n' roll's future and its name is Bruce Springsteen," he wrote. "On a night when I needed to feel young, he made me feel like I was hearing music for the first time."[7] The glowing review brought Bruce plenty of attention and made fans anxious for his next album.

It took five months to record the single "Born to Run." Music from guitars and saxophones was over-dubbed with plenty of echo and reverb to give the song a powerful sound. The explosive, thumping opening is classic rock and roll. It told the story of a young couple that needed to escape from a small town. "Born to Run" was Springsteen's first big hit. The album, with the same title, made it to No. 3 on the national charts.

His next two albums enhanced his reputation as a rocker who sang about real people with real problems, then he surprised almost everybody in 1982 with *Nebraska.* It was inspired by the work of Woody Guthrie. During his concerts, Springsteen had sung "This Land Is Your Land," which he called "just about one of the most beautiful songs ever written."[8] For *Nebraska*, he brought recording equipment into his bedroom. "I just kinda sat there: you can hear the chair creaking on 'Highway Patrolman' in particular. I recorded them in a couple of days."[9] He played the tape for the E Street Band, which then recorded new versions of the songs with him, but Bruce decided that the album sounded better without the full band. The executives at Columbia Records thought he was making a terrible mistake. They felt the songs were too slow, bleak, and depressing. *Nebraska* wasn't rock and roll; it was folk music. It took him nine months to convince them to release the album.

The title song tells the true story of a murderous rampage in the Wyoming Badlands. "Reason to Believe" is about people up against terrible problems who manage to keep hoping for a better life. "Johnny 99" is a desperate man who loses his job and winds up in jail.

It was Springsteen's next album, *Born in the USA*, that made him a superstar in 1984. The band was back, and they were rocking. The album sold more than ten million copies, and soon they were playing in huge stadiums all over the world. The title song, "I'm on Fire," "Glory Days," and "Dancing in the Dark" were played over and over on radio stations and MTV, the new music video channel.

Even President Ronald Reagan praised Springsteen, saying the two of them were trying to send the same

Twenty-two years after his first album, *Greetings from Asbury Park, N.J.*, was released, Springsteen's *Greatest Hits* album debuted at No. 1 on the charts.

message to America. Bruce was angry because he felt he had been used by Reagan in an effort to get votes. Besides, the president didn't understand "Born in the USA." It wasn't a proud song; it was a bitter, angry cry. "The guy in the song . . . comes back from Vietnam and he wants to find something new in this country," Springsteen said. But he can't even find a job. He feels betrayed by the country he risked his life for. "That search, that stand, is what the guy is screaming about."[10]

Bruce wanted to make sure his views weren't misunderstood. In his concerts, he spoke about the lives he felt were ruined by the Vietnam War. He warned his fans to think, not to blindly follow the president and other leaders. When he introduced "War," he said, "Blind faith in your leaders or in anything else will get you killed."[11]

The messages in his music were usually serious, but Springsteen and the E Street Band tried never to forget that rock and roll was supposed to be fun. They wanted to make sure their fans got their money's worth. By the mid-1980s, it wasn't unusual for their concerts to last four hours. "This kid out there, it's his money, and it's his one night," Springsteen said. "So you mustn't let him down. . . . You've got a lot to live up to when you walk out on that stage."[12] And, of course, he loved performing: "I feel like the king of the world. . . . It's the greatest feeling on earth. . . . For the moment I feel young. Young and I'm strong."[13]

Springsteen's next album came out in 1987. *Tunnel of Love* didn't address political issues; it was about the problems of being in love. Then, when he finally took a break from touring, he decided to make some musical changes. After giving each member two million dollars, he broke up the E Street Band.

Then for four years, he stayed out of the spotlight, raising a family with his wife, Patti Scialfa. He kept writing songs, and, in 1992, he had enough material to release two new albums, *Human Touch* and *Lucky Town*. "57 Channels (And Nothin' On)" was a depressing commentary on modern life, but other songs like "Better Days" and "Book of Dreams" seemed to show that Springsteen was content living the quiet life of a husband and father. "Pony Boy," in fact, was a short sweet lullaby.

Film director Jonathan Demme asked Springsteen to write a song for his 1993 movie, *Philadelphia,* the story of a lawyer (played by Tom Hanks) who dies of AIDS. Bruce responded with "Streets of Philadelphia," one of the most haunting—and popular—songs he had ever done. It earned him an Academy Award and a Grammy for Record of the Year.

While his fans waited for more music, many of them probably remember the story he told on stage during a tour in 1978:

"One day, my mom and pop, they came up to me and said, 'Bruce, it's time to get serious with your life. This guitar thing . . . it's OK as a hobby but you need something to fall back on.'" So he went to heaven to ask God if he should give up music. "And there's God, behind the drums . . . God looks at me. He says . . . 'What those guys don't understand is that there was supposed to be an Eleventh Commandment. All it said was: LET IT ROCK!'"[14]

Suggested Recordings

Greetings from Asbury Park, N.J.
(Columbia, 1973)
Born to Run (Columbia, 1975)
River (Columbia, 1980)
Born in the U.S.A. (Columbia, 1984)
Live 1975–1985 (Columbia, 1986)
Tunnel of Love (Columbia, 1987)
Human Touch (Columbia, 1992)
Lucky Town (Columbia, 1992)
Greatest Hits (Columbia, 1995)
Ghost of Tom Joad (Columbia, 1995)

Chapter Notes

Introduction

1. *Elvis* television special soundtrack, RCA Victor, 1968.

Chapter 1

1. Patricia Romanowski and Holly George-Warren, eds., *The Rolling Stone Encyclopedia of Rock & Roll* (New York: Simon & Schuster, 1995), p. 71.

2. Michael Lydon, "Let Me Hear Some of the Rock 'n' Roll Music!" insert to Chuck Berry's *The Great Twenty-eight* compact disc, Chess Records, 1984.

Chapter 2

1. Anthony DeCurtis and James Henke with Holly George-Warren, *The Rolling Stone Illustrated History of Rock & Roll* (New York: Random House, 1992), p. 25.

2. Albert Goldman, *Elvis* (New York: McGraw-Hill, 1981), p. 83.

3. Paula Taylor, *Elvis Presley* (Mankato, Minn.: Creative Education, 1975), p. 17.

4. Ibid., p. 19.

5. Peter Guralnick, insert to Elvis Presley, *The Sun Sessions CD*, RCA, 1987.

6. Ibid.

7. Goldman, p. 155.

8. Peter Guralnick, *Last Train to Memphis: The Rise of Elvis Presley* (New York: Little, Brown, 1994), p. 289.

9. DeCurtis and Henke with George-Warren, pp. 23–24.

10. *Elvis,* television special soundtrack, RCA Victor, 1968.

11. Guralnick, *Last Train to Memphis,* p. 16.

12. DeCurtis and Henke with George-Warren, p. 23.

Chapter 3

1. John Goldrosen, *The Buddy Holly Story* (New York: Quick Fox, 1975), p. 8.

2. Ibid., pp. 16–17.

3. John Goldrosen and John Beecher, *Remembering Buddy Holly: The Definitive Biography of Buddy Holly* (New York: Penguin Books, 1987), p. 29.

4. Goldrosen, *The Buddy Holly Story,* p. 41.

5. Ibid., p. 52.

6. Ibid., p. 71.

7. Fred Bronson, *The Billboard Book of Number One Hits* (New York: Billboard Books, 1992), p. 26.

8. Goldrosen, *The Buddy Holly Story,* p. 112.

9. Anthony DeCurtis and James Henke with Holly George-Warren, *The Rolling Stone Illustrated History of Rock & Roll* (New York: Random House, 1992), p. 91.

10. Philip Norman, *Shout! The Beatles in Their Generation* (New York: Simon and Schuster, 1981), p. 69.

11. Hunter Davies, *The Beatles: The Authorized Biography* (New York: McGraw-Hill, 1968), p. 69.

12. Lillian Roxon, *Rock Encyclopedia* (New York: Grosset & Dunlap, 1969), p. 236.

Chapter 4

1. Beverly Mendheim, *Ritchie Valens: The First Latino Rocker* (Tempe, Ariz.: Bilingual Press, 1987), p. 38.

2. Fred Bronson, *The Billboard Book of Number One Hits* (New York: Billboard Books, 1992), p. 675.

3. Mendheim, p. 63.

4. Ibid., pp. 96–97.

5. Ibid., p. 97.

6. Ibid., p. 108.

7. Anthony DeCurtis and James Henke with Holly George-Warren, *The Rolling Stone Illustrated History of Rock & Roll* (New York: Random House, 1992), p. 357.

Chapter 5

1. Mike Love, from his introduction to "Little Deuce Coupe" on the album, *Beach Boys Concert,* Capitol Records, 1964.

2. *Beach Boys: An American Band* video, Vestron, 1985.

3. *Beach Boys Concert.*

4. Brian Wilson, *Wouldn't It Be Nice* (New York: HarperCollins, 1991), p. 89.

5. Ibid., p. 140.

6. Ibid., p. 139.

7. Paul McCartney, insert to the Beach Boys, *Pet Sounds* compact disc, Capitol Records.

8. Michael Heatley, ed., *The Ultimate Encyclopedia of Rock* (New York: HarperCollins, 1993), p. 178.

9. Fred Bronson, *The Billboard Book of Number One Hits* (New York: Billboard Books, 1992), p. 215.

10. Wilson, p. 147.

11. *Beach Boys: An American Band.*

12. Ibid.

13. Ibid.

Chapter 6

1. Insert to Bob Dylan, *Biograph* compact disc, Columbia Records, 1985, p. 4.

2. Clinton Heylin, *Bob Dylan: Behind the Shades* (New York: Summit Books, 1991), p. 27.

3. Ibid., p. 43.

4. *Biograph*, p. 4.

5. Ibid.

6. Anthony DeCurtis and James Henke with Holly George-Warren, *The Rolling Stone Illustrated History of Rock & Roll* (New York: Random House, 1992), p. 308.

7. Ibid., p. 299.

8. Richard Williams, *Dylan: A Man Called Alias* (New York: Henry Holt, 1992), p. 178.

Chapter 7

1. Richard Williams, "Lady Soul," *Time,* vol. 91, no. 26, June 28, 1968, p. 63.

2. James T. Olson, *Aretha Franklin* (Mankato, Minn.: Creative Education, 1975), pp. 11–14.

3. Williams, p. 63.

4. Olson, p. 17.

5. Fred Bronson, *The Billboard Book of Number One Hits* (New York: Billboard Books, 1992), p. 225.

6. Ibid.

7. "The Top 100 Best Singles of the Last 25 Years," *Rolling Stone,* no. 534, September 8, 1988, p. 67.

8. Ibid.

9. "The Top 100: The Best Albums of the Last Twenty Years," *Rolling Stone,* no. 507, August 27, 1987, p. 162.

10. Mark Bego, *Aretha Franklin: The Queen of Soul* (New York: St. Martin's, 1989), p. 109.

11. Bronson, p. 664.

12. Bego, p. 119.

13. Ibid., p. 110.

Chapter 8

1. Fred Bronson, *The Billboard Book of Number One Hits* (New York: Billboard Books, 1992), p. 227.

2. Danny Sugarman, *The Doors: The Illustrated History* (New York: William Morrow, 1983), p. 11.

3. Ibid., p. 12.

4. "The Top 100: The Best Albums of the Last Twenty Years," *Rolling Stone,* no. 507, August 27, 1987, p. 84.

5. "The Top 100 Best Singles of the Last 25 Years," *Rolling Stone,* no. 534, September 8, 1988, p. 110.

6. Sugarman, *The Doors,* p. 9.

7. Ibid., p. xiv.

Chapter 9

1. John McDermott with Eddie Kramer, *Hendrix* (New York: Warner Books, 1992), p. 2.

2. Ibid.

3. Ibid., p. 17.

4. Anthony DeCurtis and James Henke with Holly George-Warren, *The Rolling Stone Illustrated History of Rock & Roll* (New York: Random House, 1992), p. 415.

5. Mitch Mitchell, *Jimi Hendrix: Inside the Experience* (New York: Random House, 1992), p. 18.

6. DeCurtis, pp. 413–14.

7. Mitchell, p. 67.

8. McDermott, p. 81.

9. DeCurtis, p. 413.

10. "The Top 100: The Best Albums of the Last Twenty Years," *Rolling Stone,* no. 507, August 27, 1987, p. 55.

11. Insert to Jimi Hendrix, *Jimi Hendrix: The Ultimate Experience* compact disc, MCA Records, 1993, p. 10.

12. "The Top 100 Best Singles of the Last 25 Years," *Rolling Stone,* no. 534, September 8, 1988, p. 128.

13. Mitchell, p. 143.

14. *Jimi Hendrix: The Ultimate Experience,* p. 21.

15. Mitchell, p. 169.

16. McDermott, p. 324.

Chapter 10

1. Mark Eliot, *Down Thunder Road: The Making of Bruce Springsteen* (New York: Simon and Schuster, 1992), p. 30.

2. Patrick Humphries, *Bruce Springsteen: Blinded by the Light* (New York: Henry Holt, 1985), p. 8.

3. Eliot, p. 30.

4. Humphries, p. 10.

5. Michael Stewart, *Bruce Springsteen* (New York: Crescent Books, 1984).

6. Eliot, p. 69.

7. Humphries, p. 23.

8. Bruce Springsteen, from his introduction to the song on the album, Bruce Springsteen and the E Street Band, *Live 1975–85*, Columbia Records, 1986.

9. Humphries, p.53.

10. Bruce Barol, *Tunnel of Love Express Tour* souvenir booklet, (San Francisco: Rock Express, 1988), p. 5.

11. Bruce Springsteen, from his introduction to the song on the album, Bruce Springsteen and the E Street Band, *Live 1975–85*, Columbia Records, 1986.

12. Humphries, p. 38.

13. Eliot, p. 240.

14. Stewart.

Further Reading

Charlton, Katherine. *Rock Music Styles: A History.* Madison, Wisc.: Brown & Benchmark Publishers, 1994.

Fornatale, Pete. *The Story of Rock 'N' Roll.* New York: William Morrow & Co., 1987.

Frankl, Ron. *Bruce Springsteen.* New York: Chelsea House, 1994.

Haskins, James S. *Black Music in America: A History Through its People.* New York: HarperCollins Children's Books, 1987.

Richardson, Susan. *Bob Dylan.* New York: Chelsea House, 1995.

Romanowski, Patricia, and Holly George-Warren, eds. *The New Rolling Stone Encyclopedia of Rock & Roll.* New York: Simon & Schuster, 1995.

Rubel, David. *Elvis Presley: The Rise of Rock & Roll.* Brookfield, Conn.: Millbrook Press, 1991.

Sheafer, Silvia. *Aretha Franklin.* Springfield, N.J.: Enslow Publishers, 1996.

Index